Entry One.

February 17ᵗʰ 2022.

Love ends.

Sadly.

Life will go on.

Terribly.

Hearts shatter.

Painfully.

People move on.

Slowly.

Time heals.

All.

Love ends.

I have had so much Love in my life. I have had so much Love in my life leave. I have had so much Love in my life stay. Sometimes I feel like life isn't real. That is a real delusion. Life is so real. Everything I have felt is real. Life is shit. That is what leads to my delusions. Life being shitty. I feel so numb sometimes from death, from Love, from all my emotions; a numbness comes. I get overwhelmed by the feeling I feel. This causes me to question if life is real. Life is real and life is shitty.

Broken.

Alone.

Numb.

Loved.

Alive.

To the point of, Numb.

Everything I experience.

Questioned.

Analyzed.

Everything I experience overwhelming me.

Forcing me to feel numb to life.

Entry Two.

February 17th 2022.

Every time.

She let me down.

Every time.

I let her down.

Toxic for each other.

Love destroying me.

Me loosing her.

Nothing left.

Nothing inside of me.

I wish I could go back and change things. Then I wouldn't of found my medications. Then I wouldn't of found the love I found for my family and friends. Then I wouldn't be who I am today. I would still be lost if I could go back and not leave that campsite that night. I would be more in Love with her. I would be less in Love with what I have had. Life worked itself out. Sure I'm still depressed every now and again. Sure I still deal with manic episodes. The important thing is I am generally stable.

Everything works out.

Everything was lost.

For a moment.

I lost even myself.

Everything will continue.

Everything will be lost.

For a moment.

I enjoy the Love, Family, and Friends.

I will miss them all.

One day.

For a moment.

Entry Three.

February 17th 2022.

If I remain silent,

Is life better?

If you don't see me,

Is life better?

I wish I could ask.

Time is leaving us behind.

Life will leave us all behind.

Never stop finding Love.

If I could just find Love and have my happily ever after that would be great. I know it won't happen anytime soon. I know it will happen again. I hope that I can be mentally stable this time. I hope that I can be more then just a work in progress. I have been in progress my entire life. I know I will never be perfect but one good year. One stable year is all I ask for.

Stable.

Going to work everyday.

Stable.

Feeling good everyday.

Stable.

Growing relationships.

Stable.

Never doing any of these things.

Stable and insane.

Insane and stable.

Entry Four.

February 17th 2022.

I have survived.

So far.

I have trusted myself.

So far.

I have lost myself.

So far.

I have broken myself.

So far.

I have pushed to hard.

So far.

So far I haven't done much that is good. I am here. That is what's important. Trusting myself hasn't always helped. At least I made my way through life so far. I will continue on finding new Love. I will continue on finding new pain.

To continue is what is hard.

I know mistakes will be made.

To continue with the pain chasing me down.

I know I have made plenty of mistakes.

To continue with the same mistakes would be insanity.

I know I will move towards new things.

Finding new pain.

Finding new mistakes.

Finding new pain.

Entry Five.

February 18th 2022.

One decision.

Can change a day.

One decision.

Can change a week.

One decision.

Can change a lifetime.

I decided to chase after something running away.

I decided to not take my medications or seek help.

I decided to drive away and run out of gas.

I made the decisions that led to me being locked away in a hospital for two months. Everyday I have to decide what I want to do. Every decision made effects my life. Every mistake is mine to own. I can only hope that I make the correct decision.

I decided to worm.

I decided to Love again.

I decided to let go of resentment.

I am moving forward making a choice everyday to stay alive.

I am not going to just survive anymore.

I will thrive.

Pain and Love along the way.

Hoping to end in peace.

Entry Six.

February 18th 2022.

I want her to call.

Still I'm silent.

I want to see her.

Still I won't move.

The chase is over.

I have found love.

Love has surrounded me in my life.

I want her to call.

Still I'm silent.

Finding Love has been hard. Mostly because I am blind. Love is right in front me. I Love my family and friends. They have been beyond good to me. I wish they knew how much I regret my ignorance. Finding Love has been hard. Mostly because I am blind. Kindness is in everyday. In kindness is Love. Strangers holding a door. People letting me pass in my car. Life allowing me to see Love again. Kindness is everywhere. I was blind. I am blind. I will be blind. Only to what I choose to be blind to. Love is one thing I will forever bring with me.

Love again.

Friends again.

Family again.

Actions are louder then words.

Show them.

Prove to them.

Never let them down.

Love again.

Remind myself of the hell I put myself in.

Love again.

Entry Seven.

February 18th 2022.

Abuse me.

Use me.

Allow me to feel again.

Numb to life's pain.

Numb to life's joy.

A blank face.

In a crowd.

Lie to myself.

This is just a phase.

Abuse me.

Use me.

Allow me to feel alive.

I'm not sure why I crave anything stimulating at certain times. I'm not sure I care if it is negative stimulation or positive. I want to feel alive that is the only thing I know. To stimulate my core. To stimulate my soul. Knowing I can be hurt at anytime. A Love that can tear me to pieces. Anything other than a mundane existence. I know I have my family and friends. It seems the only time I feel an intensity with them is when they leave. Nothing soul touching happens, until one person leaves. Then the feelings built over years or months even explode out of my soul, encompassing my heart. I'm not sure why I crave stimulation but I know I do and will. My biggest goal for this year is to remain alone.

Love me.

Call me.

Bother me.

Allow me to feel again.

Replace the numb in my soul.

Replace the numb in my mind.

Allow me to feel again.

Love me.

Call me.

Bother me.

Entry Eight.

February 18th 2022.

A sea of eyes.

Only finding hers.

Love every inch of her.

From bottom to the top.

Love her every mistake.

A sea of eyes.

Bring me to tears.

Tell her my fears.

Her Love is perfect.

Imperfect is life.

Right now life is wrong.

She brings me to tears, right now.

I can not let go. I need to let go. I need to move. I need to free my mind from the burden she has become. Help me through the hell she trapped me. A friend indeed I am a friend in need. Working life away. Working till I die. Working while I cry. I wish I could say goodbye to this part. I've even blessed. I've had less. I've felt low. I've been high. Now I wish I could say goodbye. Hang up the phone one last time. Go our separate ways.

Life feels.

Like he'll.

Like shit.

Like misery.

Life is so much more.

At least not numb.

Still living with a blank face.

At least not numb.

Entry Nine.

February 19th 2022.

Addicted to her pain.

Addicted to her love.

Loving the addiction.

Loving the chemicals.

My mind lost for a moment.

Withdrawals from her crippling me.

Giving up when I am closest.

She could be here in a month or two. I could be gone in a month or

two. I have given up on love. I have given up on her. I am done

waiting. I am going to find peace. At the very least I will find myself. A year alone should do me good. A year alone will heal me.

I can not stand the thought of falling in love again right now.

Time moving on.

Healing my wounds.

My heart opening to the lonely part of me.

Not running from but embracing myself.

Escaping one hell for another hell.

I am sure there are no easy roads left anymore.

Entry Ten.

February 19th 2022.

Take my breath away.

Find me for one more day.

Life hasn't been okay without her.

The hardest moments alone.

The worst timing I could ask for.

Life has been empty without her.

Nothing left to do.

Nothing left inside.

Life has been empty without her.

Take my breath away.

Find me for one more day.

If she could just find her way back. I would give back my everything. If she could just call one more time. I would feel like everything is fine. Help me see what is wrong. Help me be the person I know is inside. If she could just find her way back. I would be okay for another day. The hope I have is all that keeps me alive. The love I give will come back to me. I hope.

Hoping to start again.

Hoping for an actual friend.

Hoping for an end

Never getting what I need.

Never checking to feel.

Never going to trust myself.

Going through to much.

Going into a nightmare.

Going to go insane.

Entry Eleven.

February 19th 2022.

I want to be great.

At anything.

I am great at nothing.

I lack commitment.

To anything.

I want to be great and get nothing.

I don't work hard enough or long enough.

I am not good enough when I do work.

I give up so easily.

I want to be great.

At anything.

I have never been good enough. I have never even been close to enough. I have never been anything but lazy. I hope my future changes but it won't if I don't change. I hope I can change myself I have been nothing up to this point. If I don't change I won't be good enough. To develop myself into something I can love. To change my future into something I want. To be good enough for myself.

Everything changes.

Life doesn't stop for me.

Life will move on.

Time will pass me by.

Everything changes.

Everything will change.

Until I love myself and my future.

Entry Twelve.

February 19th 2022.

I want to wake up happy.

Do people ever wake up happy.

I've gone to sleep happy.

Just never awake feeling happy.

I have to work everyday for my happiness.

I want to feel alive without feeling manic.

I want a Love that puts me on the edge of my seat.

I've never been a happy person. I will never be a happy person. Few people will ever see me happy. I find it considerably more difficult to fake a smile with each passing day. I could always smile when drinking with friends. Now I don't drink and I smile less. I feel my heart becoming cold. Now I don't think that will ever change. I choose to be alone. I have never been a happy person.

Happy.

Happy is a lie.

Happy is false hope.

Happy is ignorance.

Happy is momentary.

Happy is a never

Happy is a lie.

Happy. .

Entry Thirteen.

February 19th 2022.

I will be sad.

She can use me.

I will be good.

She can use me.

I will be there.

Please use me.

Allow myself to fill her soul.

Allow myself to be place to rest her soul.

Allow myself to dry her tears if they should fall.

Please use me.

I will be here for her.

When she is ready.

I am and will always be ready.

I will always want to please people. I will always try to be there for the people I Love.

I will always be the best I can be. My illness hampers me. My mindset hampers me. My heart hampers me. Hurt feelings follow me. My emotions overwhelm me. My thoughts consume me. Wishing she was here. Knowing she may never arrive. I am and will always be ready. I will be sad.

If she arrives.

I will feel alive.

When she leaves.

Apart of my heart dies.

If she says goodbye for forever.

I will be alive.

Only to survive.

Entry Fourteen.

February 19th 2022.

Caring for those who have no one.

Attractive.

Understanding why I can't be happy.

Attractive.

Loving without holding back.

Attractive.

Showing feelings

Attractive.

She attracted me not only to her looks, but her soul. She held me close and everything was alright. I miss that but there are 8 billion people on this planet to meet. She might be one of the most attractive I've met to date. Things just didn't work out. We are to different no matter how attractive we are to each other. She changed me when she left. She changed me when we met. She attracted me to her soul. Filling a long empty void in my heart.

The void is here to stay.

The void is here to grow.

She is gone.

I am fading into oblivion.

I am falling apart at the seems.

She is gone.

Without her life will be empty.

Without her life will continue on.

I will be okay.

She will be okay.

Everything will not be okay.

That is how life should be.

I will be okay.

She is gone.

Entry Fifteen.

February 20th 2022.

The moonlit nights.

The sunset behind us..

The beach beneath us.

The birds singing to us.

The Love filled days.

The trees surrounding us.

The air filling us.

The water washing us.

The moonlit nights.

The Love filled days.

I want this all again so much. I would still go back and do it all. I want hee closer to me then ever before. I want to hear her heart in my chest. I want to hold her and tell her it was worth it. Every moment of pain worth meeting her. I will be okay or I hope I will be okay. Inside I'm aching even to this day. I want that all over again.

Pain filled nights.

Tear filled mornings.

Hopeless days.

I want it.

I want life again.

I want to live again.

With someone new.

With a Love that doesn't end in pain.

With Tears she choses to dry.

I want it all over again.

Entry Sixteen.

February 20th 2022

Loosing my mind.

Slowly.

Loosing time.

Slowly.

Passing away.

Slowly.

Each breath.

Closer to the end.

I feel like I loose my mind at least once a day. I feel like I am dying slowly. I feel like no one is out there. I wish I could have. A life without pain. A life without regret. A life lived to my fullest. My illness contains my potential. Always hindered. Always treading water. Always bobbing to stay afloat. I feel like I loose myself more each time.

Hold onto what little hope I have.

Hold onto the sanity I have.

Hold onto myself.

I will be alright one day.

I will smile one morning.

I will be okay.

Entry Seventeen.

February 20th 2022.

Could she be the one.

The one that comforts me.

The one that let's me know it's all okay.

The one that stays.

Could she be the one.

That kills me.

That destroys my heart.

That rips my soul out of me.

Could she be the one that changes everything.

I wish I knew what will happen. I wish I knew how she feels. I wish I knew her intentions. I may never know. What she wants. What she needs. What she is. So far she hasn't been good to me. I am broken as I ever have been. My family and friends the only things holding me together. I wish I could tell my future but nothing is known. Everything up in the air.

I showed her my weakness.

I showed her my strength.

Still she turned away.

I can never forget.

I can only forgive.

I will not turn back again.

She could still be a friend.

I will never forget.

I can only forgive.

Entry Eighteen.

February 20th 2022.

Her Love oppresses me.

Her Love holds me.

Only to be wasted.

Now to stay away.

No matter what will happen.

I will not give my Love to her anymore.

If this is my last breath I regret.

Giving myself to a self imposed hell.

Trapping myself in a cage of Love that wasn't real.

Oppressed by the one I Loved most.

She was a dream one day. Now a nightmare far away. A gentle kiss. A gentle soul. A gentle Love. Turned into a sea of fire by me. My misery haunting each turn. For her my heart will burn. To forget I only yearn. Never allowed to completely forget. Left alone. No answer from her phone. Left alone. In a hospital with no one and nothing to hold my heart dear. All of my fear exposed. All of my mind obliterated. All my Love quickly faded. Only to come back in waves. Until mixed into all my past grief. Never to get any relief. If only she was just a dream.

Her love must leave me.

Her heart must be forgotten.

Her mind must fade.

I only want to be okay.

I only want to leave yesterday.

I only want to be okay.

Entry Nineteen.

February 21st 2022.

Invincible is our love.

Improbable is our success.

Inevitable is our downfalls.

We will try everyday to do good.

Only to fail everyday.

Only to give up.

We will never see Love in the truest form.

Not just to die for me.

Not just to live for me.

To encompass my entire life and consume me.

We will never see Love in the truest form.

Not from her

Not from me

Love untrue.

Love with nothing to hold back.

Love that is conditional

Never to be found is true Love.

Not from her.

Not from me.

I'm not sure if I know true Love. I am not sure if I'm capable of true Love. I've been hurt.. I'm damaged goods. How can I ever have true love. My entire life is a series of disaster. One bad thing after another. If I ever find true Love. I will be happy. I fear Love is Pain and pain alone in this life. I fear I will not feel anything like Love again. I fear I will always be alone.

Her love was so real.

Her beauty was immeasurable.

I miss her today.

I will miss her tomorrow.

My life is nothing compared to her love.

Her love was so real.

Now gone forever.

Leaving me to grieve alone.

Entry Twenty.

February 21st 2022.

I hope where ever she is today she is okay.

I hope whatever she does today her love spreads.

I hope whenever I see her again I will be okay.

If time stops.

If the world ceases.

If space collapses.

I hope my soul ends up close to her Love.

I have hoped for a lot. I have received little. I always enjoy those little things I do receive. Tomorrow isn't guaranteed. Today is only a glimpse into my life. Yesterday was an eternity ago. Forgetting her Love little by little. Slowly becoming less full. My world draining empty of Love. Missing and wishing something could work out.

How can she leave me empty.

How can one goodbye be so harsh.

I would hope for better.

I should of expected less.

Everyone let's me down.

Everyone hurts.

Everyone makes mistakes.

Not hearing from her is a mistake.

Not seeing her is a regret.

Not fixing things is my fault

We all go through a lot alone.

But how could she leave me empty.

With one harsh goodbye.

Entry Twenty-one

February 21st 2022.

She was the one who lifted my head above water.

Before her broken and shattered by Life itself.

I was dying slowly and alone.

She gave me hope when I had none.

She was the one.

Now I am back to where I started alone and dying slowly.

She was the only...

For much of my life I have been drowning. Drowning in bills.

Drowning alone. At least with her I had someone next to me.

Someone that understood. Someone that loved me. I am still happy

even though I'm back to being alone. Happy to experience Love

again. Life has left me alone for do long. Any little bit of Love I

receive I am grateful for.

The only one to match my energy.

Taking not only my life in her grasp but my soul to.

The one to match my heart.

Taking my emotions and destroying all thoughts of Love

The one that abandoned me at my darkest.

Entry Twenty-two.

February 21st 2022.

I have lost my mind.

Constantly anxious.

I have lost my heart.

Constantly numb.

I have lost my life.

Constantly lost.

I have lost.

I am not feeling myself today. I haven't really felt myself for a short while. I feel little to nothing for life. I want to feel alive again. I want to have someone next to me. I am not going to find anything good sitting in Michigan. Once off of probation I will set out for the open road.

I will search.

For Love.

I will search.

For life..

I will search.

For myself.

Entry Twenty-two.

February 21st 2022.

I will be okay.

I will find a way.

Out of my past.

Into my future.

I will be okay.

If I can only stay away.

She never cared. At least not deeply. She never noticed. My Love
and open heart. She was smart. I wasn't on medication at the time.
Although still I wanted her with my entire my mind and body. I

don't care anymore. If she wanted to be in my life she would have been. I don't care. Not for another day.

I will not be okay.

I have not been okay.

Life is going to be difficult.

Without Love.

Without Trust.

How do we live as people.

Sadness replaced by anger.

I have never been okay.

Entry Twenty-three.

February 21st 2022.

My eyes heavy.

My heart cold.

My mind numb.

I could beg for her.

I could cry for her.

Instead I will move on without her.

I will find new Love.

Take down my emptiness. Take down my self pity. Take down the
pain that grows in my heart. I will make it to tomorrow. Tonight I
am filled with sorrow. Tonight I am alone again. No human contact.
No dog to comfort me. Just alone. At peace with my sorrow. At
peace with my anger. At peace with my life.

Life has been hell.

Life has been amazing.

Life can be to much.

Looking back I wish I would of tried more often.

I was often defeated by depression.

I was often misguided.

I was often alone.

Looking back I wish I would have been stable.

Life has been hard.

Life has been strangling me.

Life has been impossible.

I wish for to much.

I wish for life to be over.

I wish for a new page to turn.

Entry Twenty-three.

February 21st 2022.

I will not relent in my pursuit of Love.

Everything against me in life.

I will put up a front and fight till the bitter end.

Everything going wrong.

I will have to continue alone.

Growing only the Love close to me.

Family and Friends.

I will not relent.

I may be hell bound.

Finding misery everyday.

I will not relent.

Growing Love and Forgetting the Evil.

I will not relent.

Much of my life I have been chained down by the past evil doings done to me. I never took time to celebrate the good things. Most of the time I spent running from the evil. Instead I know now I should have been fighting the evil back every chance I could. I should have been searching for Love relentlessly. Instead I ran. I have to live with this and life has made me pay for running. Finding strength to fight will be a challenge. Finding Love worth fighting for will be a challenge. Everyday will be a fight.

Love will be my stronghold on my darkest nights.

Finding peace within the storm.

Seeing evil turn to good.

Love will be my stronghold on my darkest nights.

Finding beauty in the mundane.

Seeing dull turn to vibrant.

Love will be my stronghold.

Entry Twenty-Four

February 21st 2022.

Establishing a stronghold in Love.

Establishing relationships built on trust.

Forgetting the past.

Forgetting my pain.

Forgetting everything wrong.

Only to focus on the good.

Only to find peace, joy, and Love.

Only to receive the good in the evil.

Only to think about the future self I will become.

Much of my life has been a tremendous challenge. From school and friends. The lack of friends. The lack of good things in my life. Still with my family and few friends I have struggled through this life. Pushing onto greater things. Pushing into deeper water. The risk growing great and the reward unmeasurable. Love is all I wish to receive and pain is all I wish to forget. Life will continue to be a challenge and I will continue through to the sweet end.

Wonderful, her Love.

Wonderful, her eyes.

Wonderful, her leaving.

I am so happy.

I can see her for who she is.

I know who I am going to be.

I will take comfort in the Love of my family and friends.

Life will end, Love will end, Pain will come.

I will survive. I will grow. I will feel.

Pain will end. Growth will end. In death.

Until then I will feel alive.

Until then I will survive.

Finding Love in my family and friends.

Entry Twenty-five.

February 21st 2022.

I hope the next Love will help me when I am helpless.

The future will be good to me.

I will search for the good in me.

I find there is good in all of us.

I find there is evil in all of us.

To replace the evil with the good will be my only goal.

The future will be good.

I have high hopes I know. I will likely be let down, and that will be okay. Today has been filled with let down after let down. Tomorrow will likely be the same. I will have to struggle each and everyday. Trying to find a good moment where I can and take joy in that good moment.

I have fled from pain many times.

I should have been fighting the thing causing me pain.

I need her protection. Love hold me.

I need her next to me. Love take care of me.

I need her soul in my mind. Love consume me.

I have fled.

I have run.

Today I will fight.

Entry Twenty-six.

February 21st 2022.

Where has loyalty gone?

Where has Love gone?

Today I feel nothing.

I am numb inside and out.

Feels like I'm just going through the paces.

I want to feel alive.

I want more then just to survive.

I want so much. Receiving so little. I need to become content with what I have. I need to Love life for what it is. Good or bad I need to Love more. To not just forget the pain but to live with the pain and flourish is my goal this year. All my life I have been broken. This is the year I will mend my heart, soul, and mind. This will be the year I find peace and contentment.

I have found myself in hell.

A mind state, trapped in hell.

I have found myself.

At times forgetting my pain, relief is on the way.

I look at today as a loss.

I look at today as a opportunity for tomorrow.

I have found myself.

I have found peace.

I have lost so much.

I have to continue.

Finding more of myself tomorrow.

Entry Twenty-Seventy.

February 22nd 2022.

Where are the real ones.

Right in front of me.

Open my eyes.

Allow me to see through the past pain.

Allow me to see the future Love.

Where did the time go.

Slow my life down.

Allow me to live.

Forgive myself.

Forgive the ones that Love.

I Forgive everyone. Life raised me to forgive everyone. I do not forget anyone. I hope they forget the past me. Pain has followed me. Pain has torn my heart apart. I am sure at times the people I love do not even recognize me. I hope love can heal me. Life is in front of me. I have to do better.

With Love by my side I will be okay.

I will make to another day.

I will find myself, trapped by Love.

Hopefully in another place.

Hopefully in a different mind state.

Forgive me, I have done so much wrong.

Allow strength to spread to my friends.

I hope with Love I will be okay.

Entry Twenty-eight.

February 22nd 2022.

Deception in her heart.

Depleted in my mind.

Sucked dry by the evil she accepts.

Drained by the fight against evil in my heart.

Peace will come.

Peace will go.

Forever evil is apart of our past.

Forever Love will be in my heart.

I do not know what is in her heart, she never opened it.

I will move on fighting against the evil within me.

Forgetting the evil done to me.

Living with misery.

Living free.

Living with Love.

So many things in life are so hard to accept. The fact that all humans are capable of greatness weather it be great evil or great Love. We are all capable. Life gives us many choices. Never do we make all the right choices. I fail everyday and will continue to fail. I will always try to find Love, but I will fail as I have many times before.

Forgetting the evil in my life has been just as big of a challenge. Evil

will continue to be a challenge.

Forget my evil.

Remember my Love.

I tried my best.

Held down by mania.

Held down by depression.

Held back by myself.

Stigma haunting my future.

Life will be amazing.

Life will be terrible.

Remember that I will find Love again.

Because I search for Love.

I will not run from evil.

I will not run from my hell.

I will face it with Love in my heart.

Forget my evil.

Entry Twenty-nine.

February 22nd 2022.

Do not please people for Love.

Please them because of Love, because they Love to.

Share Love, give Love, receive Love.

Do not be afraid to Love.

Trust the next person that is next to me.

Forgive the last person that hurt me.

I have hard time with all of this. I've lost trust in so many people I Love. I've been broken. I've been afraid to Love. I can forgive, but to forget and fully move on is hard. So I'm not sure that is even truly forgiving. I will find a way and with time I'm sure life will get easier. At least that is the hope. I'm not sure so far every year has been just hard as the last. I feel lost. I feel unloved. I feel beat down. There is no writing my way out of my feelings. I can just keep going and work on changing my life. Only time will tell if I make the correct decisions. I am sure I will make mistakes. I will continue to have a hard time.

Time moves on.

With or without me.

Memories fade together.

Time will hold us accountable.

Life will be okay.

With or without me.

Entry Thirty.

February 22nd 2022.

The depth of life's beauty is unmatched.

The length of life's pain is unmatched.

Life is unmatched.

Truly living every moment.

Truly seeing every glimpse or life's beauty.

Life will always be unmatched.

I have found so many beautiful parts of life. Some of them bringing

me pain but still all the while beautiful. Nothing will compare to what truly living and enjoying life feels like. The simple gust of wind blowing her wind. The simple drop of water falling from the sky. The simplest things hold so much beauty. Nothing can compare to the beauty in life. I cherish each and every moment of life. I look forward to the next moment of pain. Because I know that pain will likely be from something beautiful like Love.

Fresh air blowing on my face during a warm spring day.

A sunset to end a long summer day.

Maple trees showing their true colors in the fall.

The good and the bad.

Beauty in every breath.

Peace will come and go.

Entry Thirty-one

February 22nd 2022.

She was flawless in the way she took my heart.

She was flawless in the way she held her beauty.

She was flawless.

Now her flaws exposed.

My flaws exposed.

Empty without her.

Empty with her.

No where to turn to.

No where to run.

My flaws eating me alive.

Love was flawless for a time. Until she got a hold of me. Now I am left with misery. I am left with myself. To carry on. To pick up my pieces. Her love left me in. Hell surrounded me. Life was dark. Life will be dark. To continue and find pieces of light.

I just need a shred of light.

Today has been hard.

I just need a moment of peace.

I just need to find a way through.

Today has been hard.

I need so much and I need to get it myself.

Seldom does life give us handouts.

Entry Thirty-two

February 22nd 2022.

I've destroyed my life more than anyone else.

I blame myself.

She left me for someone else.

I blame myself.

I've done more damage than I have good.

I can not paint myself in a pretty light.

I blame myself.

I need to stop living in my past. To start living today. To stop thinking about tomorrow. Maybe my life wouldn't be filled with tragic endings. I never let go of the end. The end holds me back. I never really know if I'll feel okay tomorrow. I know I haven't good yesterday. I know today I have felt both good and bad. Life is a struggle. Mental health is a battle. I have let go of so many things and there is so much left to let go of. I hope I find peace.

I've done terrible things.

I've wrecked my entire life.

The wrong medications.

The wrong treatments.

The wrong diagnosis.

I could blame the doctors.

It was me that chose not to speak.

It was me subdued by life.

Destroying my life was me and me alone.

Entry Thirty-Three.

February 22nd 2022.

If I never find hope.

If all I do is die alone.

My life will be a, waste.

Right now it is a waste.

I can say every night I hope to die.

I can say that but really I want to live.

I want to thrive.

Again I want to much.

I can live today.

Just live. Just Love. Just let go.

I find myself crying at night sometimes. I don't want to struggle

anymore. I don't want to wake up some nights. I could never kill

myself but to just die wouldn't be so bad. I know that's just my

mental illness. Depression kills slowly it doesn't happen over night.

Depression happens after tirelessly working for months on end. With

nothing to show for it. Depression is searching for Love with no real

Love showing up. I find myself sad but I will continue. Relief will

come one day.

I feel my pain erased for a moment.

I forget to rejoice.

I made the wrong choice.

I always let the good moments go.

To clouded by my depression to even enjoy a moment.

I feel my sorrow leave. Only to remind myself it will come another

tomorrow.

To depressed to fight for something good.

I will be okay but will my family.

Find the right medications.

Find the right therapy.

Fight to find something to rejoice in.

Entry Thirty-Four

February 22nd 2022.

My body leaving my soul behind.

My body finding numb where my mind use to be.

No body around to see me sulking in my misery.

My body giving up on my mind.

My body finding nothing inside my mind.

No body around to see my blank stare.

Help me see forget to be sad tomorrow.

Everything going to shit.

Help me forget.

I will be without a second job soon enough. Life will be hard. I will not have enough money. O have no real opportunity to find a better job. I could go back to milking cow's but I would hate that. I could find some other type of farm work. I just don't see my life being very joyful. This year will be a huge challenge. So much is up in the air.

Anxiety growing.

Unrest in my soul.

Depression growing.

Hope fading.

Will I be ever find my place.

Will I ever be okay.

Someone is out there.

Just trying to survive like me.

Both of us feeling hopeless.

The world turning its back.

My mind numb.

My body broken.

My soul lost.

Entry Thirty-Five.

February 23rd 2022.

How long will I be alone?

How long will I long for Love.

I have been left to toil in the mud.

I have been left behind by Life.

How long must I suffer in this life.

Waking up in a bed of sorrow.

Thinking about my future gives me no hope.

How long will I be alone?

One day alone seems like an eternity.

I cry out and no hears my cries. I wake up sad again. I think about the future and know it will be filled with more sorrow. No hope in my heart. Everything sucked dry today. I know think about the positive. Fight through this. For how long must I fight. Everyday is a challenge. Every moment is draining my hope slowly. I cry out and get no reply.

I will continue alone.

I must continue to search for good.

No matter how alone.

There is something in this world for me.

My little slice of peace must be found.

I will continue with my sorrow.

Looking for hope in tomorrow.

Knowing I very well may be alone for years to come.

Everything in my life going wrong.

For my family I will remain strong.

Entry Thirty-Six

February 23rd 2022.

I sleep in silence.

I live in silence.

Silent pain floods my dreams.

Dreams of her face from years ago.

Dreams of her smile seldom seen.

Dreams of my life not alone.

Living in a silent depression.

The life being drained from me.

This moment is all I have.

The moment is what it is.

My mind silent.

My heart silent.

Trapped by life.

I live in silence.

Finding silence, is not finding peace. Finding peace can be silent. Finding my heart surrounded by silence. Finding my heart alone, aching for a new Love, aching for a new life. Receiving nothing but words that are suppose to comfort me. Life will work itself out. The sun is still shining. The wind still blowing. None of these words comfort me anymore. The only thing I can take comfort in is the future. Today is a pile of rubbish. Today is lonely. Yesterday was the same. Tomorrow still isn't known. I hope tomorrow I awake with joy instead of dreams of loneliness.

So far miserable.

So far barely able.

So far only alone.

Life isn't about where I began.

Life isn't a competition.

Life is about where I want to be.

I will attempt another day.

If I am only let down.

If I am only alone at night.

I will attempt another day.

Eventually one day I will be awakened by Love.

Entry Thirty-Seven.

February 23rd 2022.

Allow truth to set my heart free.

Finding Love where Love shouldn't be.

Swimming in a sea of misery.

Rescued by Love alone.

Nothing in front of me.

Nothing behind me.

Nothing inside of me.

Rescued by Love alone.

Allow truth to set my heart free.

Find Love in the sea of misery.

Swim onward and find joy.

One day soon.

Life will make sense to me.

Until then I fight to keep my head above water.

Insanity following my every move.

I surely can not keep in front of Life for long.

Everything will go wrong.

Allow truth into my heart.

Allow me to find her Love.

Allow me to cherish the good moments.

I know this depression is just a phase. I know this pain will fade. I know I will be alone for a good time to come. I will allow the good into my heart, even if I'm alone. My loneliness will not define who I am or who I want to be. The lack of Love is painful. How much Love does my mind need to heal? When will these feelings of pain fade? I will continue to move forward alone in my heart, alone in my mind. I will become who I need to be in order to share my Love, instead of consuming the Love around me.

My mind destroying what I care about.

My heart consuming the Love nearest to me.

My eyes blinded by my past pain.

I will continue trying to give out Love.

Trying to give out Joy.

To see her smile for a moment.

To see her Love pain free.

I will try not to destroy what I care about.

I will try my hardest to give more Love then I receive.

I will try.

Entry Thirty-Eight.

February 23rd 2022.

I've been shaken.

I've been broken.

Life has tested me.

I've failed time and time again.

Yet still I'm here.

Waiting for the next test from life.

My current test is that of loneliness.

I have fought to stave off my loneliness.

Yet I have failed.

Yet I have succeeded.

Everything is a challenge.

To wake up from a dream of her face.

To go to sleep with her on my mind.

No one in particular.

Longing for a companion.

I've been shaken..

I've been broken..

I will continue to struggle.

Reminded or Love in the past.

Reminded of my loneliness today.

I know door dash is not the healthiest job for me. I just don't see any other option for me. I can not stick with a schedule like I had at Applebee's. Sure overtime and guaranteed pay was nice but working two weeks in a row was not. I know I will always struggle finding meaning in my life. I am just not very good at looking at the positive. I try to stay positive, Life makes that difficult. I have to be real with my situation in order to change. I know I will find a way through if I continue to struggle.

Without Love I will struggle.

Without Love my heart cries out

Without myself I am lost.

I will forget my past self.

Not bogged down by the pain of past life.

Forgetting all the times I have been let down.

I have been led astray many times.

Getting further from my goals.

This time may not be any different.

This time may end in failure.

This time I will fight with all my strength.

Without Love. I am lost. Without pain. I forget.

CPSIA information can be obtained
at www.ICGtesting.com
Printed in the USA
BVHW051721080223
658145BV00013B/703